DISCUSSION PAPER 58

I0026758

THE ELITE AS A CRITICAL FACTOR
IN NATIONAL DEVELOPMENT
The Case of Botswana

DAVID SEBUDUBUDU & PATRICK MOLUTSI

NORDISKA AFRIKAINSTITUTET, UPPSALA 2011

Indexing terms:
Botswana
Ruling class
Elite
Leadership
Governance
Political stability
Democracy
Economic performance
Development planning
Economic and social development

Language checking: Peter Colenbrander

ISSN 1104-8417

ISBN 978-91-7106-695-4

© The authors and Nordiska Afrikainstitutet 2011

Production: Byrå4

Print on demand, Lightning Source UK Ltd.

Contents

Acknowledgement Note

The initial research was part of the Leaders, Elites and Coalitions Research Programme (LECRP) that brought together researchers and policy makers. The programme was jointly managed by the World Bank, Australian Agency for International Development (AusAID), UK Department for International Development (DFID) and United States Agency for International Development (USAID). We wish to express our sincere thanks to the LECRP for allowing us to publish a revised version of the paper.

Foreword

This Discussion Paper examines the role of the coalition between political leaders and elites as a critical factor in Botswana's development. It provides a historically grounded analysis of the evolution, nature and politics of this ruling coalition, and the ways its politics and governance style have contributed to the successful developmental project in Botswana. Part of its analysis focuses on the development of the ruling elite, their socio-cultural and educational roots and trajectories, and how this shaped coalition-building and networking among individuals that were to constitute the future leaders of the country and their collective vision for national development. Sebudubudu and Molutsi explore the anatomy of the 'grand coalition' that underpinned the Botswana development project, providing explanations for one of Africa's success stories in terms of economic growth and political stability. Of note is their analysis of the factors of leadership, the balancing of ethnic, racial, and regional interests within the ruling coalition in successfully defining the multi-ethnic and multi-racial character of Botswana's 'development' elite. Another important point that is carefully unpacked by the paper is the deliberate and careful negotiation of the ruling pact between various competing factions of the elite, particularly the traditional and the modern factions. The paper explains how the opposing worldviews of the traditional leaders and modern political elite were managed, to institutionalize the power of the latter over the former without any major conflict. It also shows that rather than 'completely losing out', the political elite successfully blended in aspects of traditional institutions into modern structures of governance. Examples include the use of the traditional assembly or *Kgotla* as a forum for broad consultations, consensus-building and adjudication of local cases. This explains how traditional institutions have been included and successfully co-opted by the post-colonial elite in a broad ruling coalition. It is thus an example of the blending involved as a political strategy of coalition-building and inclusiveness by an elite keen on focussing its attention on social harmony and consensus around a vision of national development and stability. Considerable attention is devoted in the paper towards the emergence of elite-led political parties in Botswana and their role in building a post-colonial Botswana ruling coalition along broadly consensual lines. The reasons why the Botswana Democratic Party (BDP) was the party was the most successful in building the grand governing coalition is laid bare, particularly with regard to the privileged background of its leaders, its ideological moderation, the ways it strategically dealt with ethnic and racial issues in an inclusive manner, and the establishment of an All Party Consultative conference in the late-1990s as a forum for consultation and building consensus on several national issues. Apart from the political, the paper analyzes the economic basis of Botswana's development. It shows how through economic prudence, state control and management of land and mineral resources, and a strategic partnership between the state, an agrarian elite, labour, international investors and the private sector Botswana was able to transform its natural resources into source of substantial national wealth and development. The paper succeeds in providing empirical and substantive evidence to demonstrate that the agency of the elite in creating a particular kind of politics and democratic developmental state has been a crucial element in making Botswana a success story of African development and political stability. It is a story that will interest development planners and workers, scholars, policy makers and the general reader.

Cyril Obi
Senior Researcher
The Nordic Africa Institute

Abstract

This study analyzes the important role of the elite and leadership coalitions in the emergence of a developmental state in Botswana. It examines the origins, nature and politics of Botswana's leaders, particularly the elite and the ways in which they contributed to the development of the country over the past four decades following the country's independence in 1966. The perspective adopted in this study focuses on both formal and informal settings and arenas of decision-making, planning and governance; on political, economic and social interactions (for instance between traditional and modern leaders) and on inter-ethnic and inter-racial ethnic coalition building. The analysis undertaken in this paper transcends the standard institutional and policy-focussed approaches by drawing attention to the basis of elite and coalitional strategies and decisions regarding national development policy, and thereby contributing to Botswana's emergence as an African developmental success story. The study examines how the interactions of leaders and elites in forming cross-cutting coalitions were shaped and framed by local factors and institutional contexts. In this regard, it relied on secondary and primary sources, including interviews with some key actors who played or still play key roles in the political, bureaucratic, social, traditional systems and institutions that continue to contribute to the reproduction of the ideology and practices of the country's founding fathers. The study concludes that key among the elite coalitions were those that were established across traditional-modern sectors, across political parties, across the ethnic-racial divisions, across the public-private sectors, across employer-employee relations as well as state and non-state actors in business and non-governmental sectors. This study of the leaders, elites and coalitions suggests that Botswana achieved what it did out of carefully designed and managed political strategies. The specific geo-political and ethno-historical situations of the country were and continue to be important additional structural factors, but were not on their own critical determinants of the successful policy and strategy. Instead, it was the leadership's conscious effort to shape Botswana into what it is today – a functioning democratic 'developmental state' – that has been of primary importance (Leftwich, 1995). However, as in any society, there remain some challenges and threats which have been dealt with through the medium of an institutional and policy framework that was locally devised, legitimate and appropriate based on broad consultation, inclusive participation and consensus.

Introduction

Botswana is regarded by some as a successful 'developmental state' (see Leftwich, 1995; Edge, 1998; Tsie, 1998; Maundeni, 2001; Taylor, 2003; Sebudubudu, 2005). From acute poverty at independence in 1966, Botswana has become one of Africa's developmental success stories. Most international and national development indicators/country assessments show that Botswana is one of the top performers on the continent. Why has Botswana been so successful? What key factors account for its good performance in an economically challenging African environment where poverty, failure of democratic institutions and the corrupt practices of the leadership most times become contributory factors in otherwise resource rich economies falling prey to violent conflict and untold misery?

This study takes a close look at the role of social and political actors and coalitions, particularly the elite in successfully propelling Botswana along a developmental path. A lot has been written about Botswana's democracy, her economic stability, her low levels of corruption and the unique management skills of the leadership, particularly when it comes to using diamond revenues to promote broad based development programmes that have helped make the country a stable middle income economy.

The Developmental State as a Conceptual Framework

The nature of its politics is an important factor in the development of a country. Politics is among other factors in turn influenced by the character and relationships between leaders or members of the governining elite. These relationships go a long way in defining the political system, either in democratic or non-democratic terms, or developmental or non-developmental terms. The vision, commitment and politics of the leadership also go a long way in shaping the political economy and defining the character of the state. In other words, the state, democracy, development and public policy are products of practical and deliberate strategies adopted by the leaders of each country. Leftwich (1996:17) succinctly summarised this position as follows:

> ...good governance and democracy are not mere components which can be inserted into any society at any point in its development, like a socket or valve. On the contrary, both good governance and democracy depend crucially on the character and capacity of the state which, alone, can institute and insist on it. And the capacity of a state to deliver good governance and protect democracy is in turn a function of its politics and its developmental determination.

Not all democratic states are successful developmental states and not all successful developmental states are democratic. Around the world democratic states are considered democratic in the sense of giving primacy to the rule of law and promoting and protecting political institutions that permit broad participation through regular elections and a parliamentary system of government. Some democracies particularly in the developing world however have existed under conditions of general poverty and overall conditions of social crisis. Countries such as South Korea, China, Singapore and Malaysia which are successful developmental states have not been always considered 'democratic'. Although some of these including Singapore and Malaysia have over the years opened up their political systems, they were for the most part of their major developmental transition in the 1980s quite authoritarian in their politics. China remains across the world, a typical successful non-democratic developmental state which has reduced poverty, brought about socio-economic transformation and accumulated a lot of wealth.

The characteristics of a developmental state as used in this paper refers to the leaders deliberate decisions to work together to achieve a particular developmental vision for their society, and their ability to manage conflict, device strategies for cooperation, negotiation and compromises designed to avoid alienation and disgruntlement among significant sections of the key elite.

The Cultural and Historical Context

The political and economic environments of Botswana have undoubtedly facilitated policies that impacted positively on the quality of life of the majority of the population. The income per capita of Botswana has increased from a meagre US$ 80 at independence in 1966 to US$ 5,600.00 in 2007, according to World Bank estimates. The country has consequently emerged from among the poorest twenty five nations in the 1960s to become one of the upper middle income economies in the world. Politically, Botswana has escaped the scourge of military coups, and is an example of a stable multiparty democracy marked by order succession of its political leadership. The country boasts a good human rights record, and has been cited in many circles as a model of good governance in Africa.

The social development record of Botswana, which has had positive impact on the quality of life, has also been notable. The country's literacy rate has grown from below 25% of the adult population to over 90% in 2007. Access to primary education stood at over 90% while that of the three year junior secondary was 100% in 2007. Transition to senior secondary has increased from below 30% in the late 1990s to 67% in 2008. Access to tertiary education, though still low in comparison with some of Botswana's neighbours – especially middle income ones such as Mauritius, Namibia and South Africa – has been growing steadily, from 7% in 2005 to 11.4% in 2008.

In the health sector, Botswana has done well in reducing maternal and child mortality and has reduced communicable and environment-related diseases. Above all, Botswana has responded decisively to the scourge of HIV/AIDS. The spread of HIV infection has been significantly curtailed and mother-to-child HIV transmission has been dramatically reduced. Access to clean and drinkable water, to basic food needs and to sanitary facilities has been significantly improved, even though the levels differ between households and from one district to another. Over 95% of the population lives within 15km of a health facility. Life expectancy increased to 65 years in 1991 up from 48 at independence, though this has been reversed to 56 with the advent of HIV/AIDS. However, the government has put in place measures to mitigate this disease.

Assessing Botswana on the basis of the core indicators of health (reduced mortality), education (basic literacy rate) and economic performance (increased per capita income), good leadership has enabled the country to record impressive achievements. Botswana has also used its mineral wealth to improve infrastructure so that there now exists some 10 000 km of paved road compared to the 10km it inherited at independence. Domestic employment has increased from 29 000 at independence to 550 000 in 2006, as many people have found jobs in government, local government, the parastatal and private sectors. Employment levels have gone up significantly, as shown by the overall drop in the unemployment rate from 23% in 1994/1995 to 17.6% in 2005/6. All these achievements are not simply the result of sound policies but, more fundamentally, flow from the solid political and institutional foundations for growth established by the leaders and elites at the time of independence and progressively sustained ever since.

All the foregoing are clear indicators of the nature of the Botswana state and its determination to promote inclusive politics and development. The question that remains is why and how did Botswana state acquire this character?

The Nature of Botswana Elite – The Critical Success Factor

Botswana's elite is unique in a number of ways. Firstly, being predominantly of one Tswana stock, it has a common cultural background, one language and a common socio-cultural orientation. Secondly, because many of the elite studied together in institutions outside the country and/or in a few elite schools within the country, they developed a common political and social value system. And third, their foreign studies in Southern Africa and abroad facilitated their interactions with foreign students which gave them a broad world outlook. Towards the end of its rule, the British Protectorate Administration developed nascent political institutions that brought modern and traditional elites, African and European leaders together and helped foster a common understanding. Trust between key actors who inherited the postcolonial state also contributed to forging what were otherwise potentially hostile relations between different elites. The personal experiences and roles of key leaders, such as Seretse Khama, Quett Masire and others in elite coalition building cannot be underestimated.

The schoolmate friendships that developed in South African institutions such as Tiger Kloof, Fort Hare and Lovedale between leaders in opposite sides of the political divide like the late Moutlakgola Nwako of the ruling Botswana Democratic Party (BDP) and the late Kenneth Koma of the opposition Botswana National Front (BNF), among others, and for the second generation during their studies in Lesotho and Swaziland (in the then joint university) became handy in the formation of key state and social institutions. For instance, many of the leaders married their classmates or friends of their sisters, brothers and cousins, invited one another into political parties, formed community-based organizations together, recruited one another into the public service and even formed private business investment agencies as friends, colleagues and inter-ethnic/racial elite groups. At home, the only university and the limited number of technical schools around the country ensured that generations of the elite went through the same educational system and institutional experience. Here too, a broad-based schoolmate camaraderie evolved which later enabled easy networking relationships. In this way, education was a key factor and underpinned the coalitions that emerged later, and contributed to Botswana's development (Interviews with Gobe Matenge on 19 December 2008; Peter Letlhogonolo Siele on 31 December 2008; Botsweletse Kingsley Sebele on 10 January 2009; Festina Bakwena on 11 February 2009; Patrick Molutsi on 22 February 2009; Binkie Kerileng on 26 February 2009; Lt Gen. Mompati Merafhe on 9 March 2009).

Familiarity with each other enabled the emerging Botswana national elite to form a successful "grand coalition" which in turn contributed to political, social and economic stability. The 'grand coalition' has become a critical success factor in Botswana and stands in sharp contrast with countries such as Burundi, Ethiopia, Kenya, Lesotho, Malawi, Rwanda, Somalia, Sudan, Zambia, Zimbabwe, and many other African countries, where ethnic and racial conflict and infighting created unstable governments and hampered development. Instead, the larger political strategy of balancing regional, ethnic and racial interests enabled the Botswana elite to work together in harmony and for a common development agenda which has seen the country transform from one of the poorest in the world to a middle income country in the twenty first century. The coalitions took various forms and were both formal and informal. In particular political party co-operation, public–private sector partnerships, traditional-modern institutional collaboration, and other business groupings of friends are evident throughout the postcolonial history of the country. The government, the private sector, the labour movement and the non-governmental sector gave expression to this grand coalition when, in 1996, the then second president of Botswana, President Quett Masire, established a non-statutory consultative forum called a High Level Consultative Council (HLCC).

The Context: Multi-ethnic and Multi-racial Character of the Botswana's Developmental Elite

While it has been noted that Botswana's leaders and elite played a critical role in the country's development, there were other contributory contextual factors in its success story. The first of these unique features was the country's peculiar ethnic structure and the nature of its colonial history. Unlike many African countries, Botswana has no central monarchy or a single dominant ethnic group. This does not mean all ethnic groups are of the same size. It only means that the big ones are not big enough to dominate others in the political, social or economic sense. This situation created an environment like the one in some parliaments elsewhere where there is a multiplicity of parties of different strengths in parliament and none enjoys an absolute majority. In such situations, as evident in Italian and Israeli experiences among others, the small parties gain "inflated importance" as they are needed to balance majorities in parliament. This analogy fits Botswana's ethnic structure well and it was the need to minimise conflict that generated an inclusive political strategy amongst the first generations of the country's post-colonial leaders (Interviews with Goboletswe Ketsitlile on 29 December 2008; Otlaadisa Koosaletse on 31 December 2008; Patrick Molutsi on 22 February 2009; Binkie Kerileng on 26 February 2009).

Botswana is made up of a number of Tswana-speaking groupings which constitute the dominant socio-cultural and political pattern of the society. They each have their chief and a distinct territory. During the Protectorate Administration era, the chiefdoms were established in eight "Native Reserves". These were the Reserves of Bangwato, Bakwena, Bangwaketse, Batawana, Bakgatla, Balete, Barolong and Batlokwa (later called eight main tribes in the constitution). During the 1920s the Protectorate Administration formed an advisory body called the African Advisory Council, constituted by the chiefs from the eight Native Reserves and a few 'educated' persons from each of the chiefdoms/reserves. Outside the reserves were a number of other groups, some not of Tswana origin. These were living in what were called Crown Land, largely in the Kalahari and North East parts of the country. Among these groups were people of Afrikaner origins in places such as Ghantsi, Bokspit and along the Molopo River on the border between Botswana and South Africa; and the Kalanga people on the Botswana-Zimbabwe border in the north and northeast. Within the reserves, there were several distinct ethnic groups including Babirwa, Bapedi, Baherero, Basarwa, Batswapong in the Bangwato reserves and Bakgalagadi, Basarwa, Bakaa and others in the Bakwena and Bangweketse reserves. Batawana Reserve was perhaps the most ethnically diverse. Other than the Batawana, it included Bayei, Barotse, Humbukushu, Baherero, Basubia and Basarwa. Outside the reserves and crown lands were the white settlers living predominantly in freehold land (then about 5% of the total land area) in the eastern parts around Lobatse, Gaborone, the Tuli Blocks and Francistown area. The new leaders of Botswana, therefore, had the challenge of including all the leaders of different groups within and outside reserves, the white settlers of English and Afrikaner origin, as well as minority groups of Indian origin found scattered across different parts of the country.

Given this diversity the constitutional talks of 1963 were rather challenging. On the one hand, the new state had to include all leaders of different groups while, on the other hand, it had to maintain the stability of the native reserves which were the basis of chiefs' rule and grip on the society. Would the different racial groups feel counted? Or would they feel excluded? These questions are addressed in the following sections.

Two Elites with Contrasting Value Systems

At independence, national leaders were not only concerned with ensuring that leaders of the different ethnic and racial groups were included in the grand political coalition, but also needed to find an acceptable and respected role for the traditional elite (Interviews with Elmon Tafa on 2 February 2009; Leach Tlhomelang on 3 February 2009; XYZ on 11 February 2009; Patrick Molutsi on 22 February 2009; Lt Gen. Mompati Merafhe on 9 March 2009). The new elite and traditional elite however represented two contrasting world views – one traditional-authoritarian and the other Christian-liberal and tending towards a democratic system of government. These were evident in the Advisory Council which had brought the modern and traditional elites together as advisers to government.

The minutes of the African Advisory Council in the 1930s and 1940s and its successor Legislative Council in 1950s and early 1960s show the contrasting perspectives between traditional leaders and the emerging new western-educated elite (see for instance, Fawcus, 2000; Molutsi, 1983 and Parsons, 1974; and 1985). These tensions were later succinctly captured by Quett Masire, Botswana's second President and a former member of the Legislative Council which negotiated the new independence constitution. In his autobiography, Masire (2006) has much to say about how his Chief hated and frustrated him simply because he was educated, modern and very successful in farming. In his book Masire further explains why he and other members of the educated elite rejected the chiefs and feared their possible direct and active role in party politics. He also spells out why and how they hastened to transfer control of communal/tribal land from the chiefs to the newly established land boards. Indeed, the relationship between the new elite and traditional elite was well captured in the first manifesto of the Bechuanaland Democratic Party (now Botswana Democratic Party) of 1965 (Bechuanaland Democratic Party, 1965). It stated that "the

Bechuanaland Democratic Party stands for a *gradual* but *sure* evolution of a national state in Bechuanaland, to which tribal groups will, while they remain in existence, take a secondary place. This is an unavoidable development, an evolutionary law to which we must yield to survive, or resist and disappear as a people" (Bechuanaland Democratic Party, 1965: 5). As Fawcus (2000:91) noted, "the Democratic Party leaders had their differences with the chiefs, but were aware of the strength of tribal institutions and knew that, when the time came to devise the territory's … constitution, *an accommodation* would have to be worked out between the chiefs and the politicians".

The other personal story of a relationship which symbolises different and contrasting world views between the new elite and traditional leaders was that of Seretse Khama and his uncle and guardian Tshekedi Khama, between 1948 and 1957/8. The spark came from the well-documented story of the marriage of Seretse Khama, heir to the Bangwato chiefdom, to a white lady while studying in the United Kingdom. Seretse was determined to keep his wife and bring her to Bechuanaland against strong objections from his uncle – and Regent – Tshekedi Khama, the leaders of South Africa and British colonial leaders in the region who were all opposed to multiracial marriages at the time. Although a fairly educated and receptive person to a lot of western ideas, Tshekedi did not accept the idea of the chieftaincy of Bangwato going to heirs of a "mixed marriage". This incident divided Bangwato into two camps and ultimately both Tshekedi and Seretse decided to renounce their right to the chieftaincy of Bangwato. Other cases of conflict between traditional versus modern elites were reported in other reserves, for example among the Barolong and Bakwena.

These two life stories of Quett Masire and Seretse Khama, the two (then) strongest chiefs in the country, each coming from two of the largest Tswana groups in the country, offer two important lessons of how modern Botswana was formed around the settlement of the tense relationship between the new elite on the one hand and the traditional conservative elite on the other. How were these reconciled and by whom? These are the key questions answered below by (a) the coalitions formed at Constitutional Talks of 1963 in Lobatse town; (b) the formation of political parties to the exclusion of chiefs; and (c) the establishment of democratic local government institutions, immediately after independence, taking away the powers of the chiefs but incorporating them into the new and democratic local government system.

Constitutional Talks of 1963 – A Defining Moment for the New Botswana

The Constitutional Talks held in the town of Lobatse in 1963 were in many ways a defining moment for the future of Botswana. First, they were to conclude that Bechuanaland Protectorate, like the other two High Commission Territories of Lesotho and Swaziland in Southern Africa, would indeed not become incorporated into South Africa as the latter's leaders had been trying to arrange since the 1920s against the wishes of the Tswana chiefs. The Constitutional Talks settled the issue of incorporation once and for all. By so doing, the Talks also decided that the country would become an independent state in a few years. It indeed attained self-rule in 1965 and full independence in 1966. Secondly, the Talks defined what type of state it would be in terms of whether or not the Chiefs would be the key inheritors of the new national state, whether it would be a coalition of the new elite with the chiefs or just the former alone at the helm of state power (Interview with Gobe Matenge on 19 December 2008). In the event, it was a coalition of the multi-ethnic and multi-racial elite of a moderate character which emerged as the inheritor of the new independent Botswana.

The Lobatse Constitutional Talks were a landmark in other respects. In the first place they pitted different key stakeholders against each other. Present among them were the chiefs, the new elite (educated Batswana of different ethnic groups), the nationalist leaders (mainly the Botswana Peoples Party (BPP)), the leaders of the white settler community and some religious leaders. In fact, these were negotiations and to call them talks implies that the discussions were smooth when they were not. During the Talks it emerged that the BPP with its radical urban politics modelled around the Pan Africanist Congress of South Africa and the African National Congress (ANC) was unacceptable to all the other representatives. The chiefs, the white settler leaders, the moderate new elite and the Protectorate Administrators found the BPP rather divisive. That the BPP could not be a key player in the new coalition was set out at the Constitutional Talks as shown below.

The other group of negotiators were the chiefs. The leaders here were Bathoen Gaseitsewe, Linchwe II of Bakgatla and Neale Sechele of Bakwena, among others. The chiefs' position was that they would be the leaders of the new state. Their view was that they were the legitimate representatives of the different communities in the country. They also saw their role as carrying on what they had been doing in the African Advisory Council and subsequently the Legislative Council. After detailed and critical discussions, the chiefs' final position was that they should be placed in a supreme House of Chiefs above the National Parliament. This House would be similar to the British House of Lords.

In the chiefs' view, the new elite were determined to usurp their powers and they were not prepared to let them achieve this goal. It was not only the new elite who were uncomfortable with the chiefs proposal but the BPP, the white settler leaders and the Government Officials were not convinced that the chiefs were ready to be national leaders of a modern state. Like the BPP, the chiefs lost much in the Lobatse Talks. The final agreement gave them a mere advisory role in the Lower House of Chiefs and further barred them from playing an active role in politics. Clearly the chiefs were bruised by this conclusion and, as shown in the next sections of this study, would continue the battle for power at the regional level. It was the disappointment with the outcome of the Talks put against subsequent local government reforms that further disempowered the chiefs, which made Bathoen II of Bangweketse resign his chieftaincy to join the opposition in politics in 1969.

Having eliminated both the radical politics of the BPP and the conservative traditional position of the chiefs, the new leadership was poised to spell out the nature of the new state. The challenges before them were to assure first the leaders of the white settler communities and other foreign minorities that they would remain accepted in the new state. The second challenge was how different communities would be accommodated, including those outside the native reserves. In this way, the Talks were a defining moment again because it was in light of the challenges just outlined that the issues of the bill of rights, freedom of speech, multi-party democracy and a multi-racial society of equals before the law were resolved. The constitution was thereby collectively defined by the first grand coalition of the new leadership.

In part, the preparatory work for a democratic state had been hatched in the Legislative Council that was established in 1959, and which brought together the leaders of different groups including the chiefs. The Legislative Council (Legco) provided a forum for familiarisation amongst emerging leaders for it was here that they got to know each other better. In the course of its meetings between 1959 and 1963 a new moderate Botswana Democratic Party (BDP) was formed, mainly by members of the Legco.

Political Parties as Grand Coalitions of Elites

The political parties were formed by identifying key individuals from each ethnic and/or racial grouping. Our interviews show that the first serious political parties succeeded or failed on the basis of their strategic alliances, or lack thereof. The history of different political parties is outlined in the following sections.

a. The Botswana Peoples Party (BPP)

The Bechuanaland Peoples Party (BPP), the first political party formed in 1960, for instance, was led by individuals from the relatively larger ethnic group of Bangwato but included at the Central Committee level leaders of ethnic minority groupings from Francistown, North East and Okavango in the North Western parts of the country. However because of its radical anti-colonial stance, the BPP was racially exclusive of the white settler leaders in the country. The BPP also failed to penetrate other main ethnic groupings in the country. For instance, it was not able to gain visibility or support in the large chiefdoms of Bakwena, Bangwaketse and Barolong in the south east. However, the BPP was more visible in the towns and areas close to white settler farms such as Ghanzi,

Gaborone, Lobatse and Francistown. It was also able to succeed among the Bak-gatla chiefdom whose chief was quite a radical character.

The BPP subsequently broke into three factions on the eve of independence. Its leader Kgalemang Motsete, from the Bangwato chiefdom, remained with a much weaker faction; while Phillip Matante and Motsamai Mpho went in different directions. Mr Mpho subsequently re-named his faction the Botswana Independence Party (BIP). At the first election in 1965 the BPP (Matante) was only able to win three seats from Francistown, Northeast and Bakgatla constituencies, while BIP did not win any seats. The evidence from the BPP case study suggests very clearly that its radical political ideology was a factor that made the party fail to form a successful coalition with leaders from the other ethnic and racial groupings in the country. In fact, the BPP remains a marginal political force in Botswana up till the present.

b. The Botswana Democratic Party (BDP)

The Botswana Democratic Party (BDP) was established in 1962 and was led predominantly by members of the Legislative Council. This was a body formed by the British Protectorate Administration in the late 1950s and composed of the leading chiefs, educated Africans and leaders of the white settler communities in the country. The BDP learnt some lessons from the BPP's failures. First, the BDP was initiated by strategically placed and popular individuals from their individual ethnic and racial groupings. Secondly, the BDP leaders had among them men from royal families who were either chiefs or relations of chiefs. Also important among them were the self-made emerging leaders such as Masire, Tsheko, Tsoebebe, Ngwako and others. Also critical at this stage was the fact that the BDP recruited the leaders of the white settler communities among them were Messrs Russell England, Steenberg, Haskins, Blackbeard and others.

The BDP, unlike the BPP, was a grand coalition of the strategically well-placed and privileged leaders from the very beginning. It was its strategic placing and the fact that its formation had been facilitated by the Protectorate Administration that gave the BDP its moderate ideological stance and, indeed, also defined its grand political position in addressing both racial discrimination, socialist and African socialism ideologies of the 1950s and 1960s. The BDP was able to make a successful appeal to the wider sections of the population and won the first election in 1965 with 28 of the 31 seats in the first Parliament. Since then the BDP's grand coalition of ethnic and racial leaders (many of whom were also related to the traditional ruling families of different ethnic groups) has managed to win all of the past nine elections held every five years in the country since 1965 with large majorities.

This coalition at the political level has been manifest in the composition of both the Cabinet and the Public Service. Different generations of Cabinets have been made up of individual leaders from different ethnic and racial groups. Some of our respondents narrated the case of Mr. Masire, the second President, who not only selected his first Vice President from the Bangwato ethnic group (the largest ethnic group of the first president) but also went out of his way to nominate a Kalanga as a specially elected member of Parliament and another Kalanga as an Assistant Minister (Interviews with Gobe Matenge on 19 December 2008; Otlaadisa Koosaletse on 31 December 2008). As a historical political strategy, the regional and ethnic balancing of the Cabinet however declined during the Presidency of Mr. Mogae, the third President of the country.

Mr Mogae appointed his Vice President and a significant number of his Ministers from his own Bangwato ethnic group. That this was not an accepted practice was shown by the media outcry against this perceived departure from the past practice as pointed out by several newspapers. At another level however, President Mogae made significant changes in the Constitution to accommodate simmering discontent by some ethnic minorities who felt under-represented in the House of Chiefs and discriminated against by sections of the Constitution which made reference to some ethnic groups as major and others as minor. He set up a nationwide consultative process which resulted in the reforms which changed those clauses in the Constitution and allowed for the creation of an expanded House of Chiefs. Although he has retained the Mogae mode of Cabinet appointment, the current President Khama (son of the first President, Seretse Khama) has retained some significant balancing in the Cabinet by appointing an Afrikaner as the Minister of agriculture (Interview with Patrick Molutsi on 22 February 2009).

Although there are no quotas of the Nigerian type in the Public Service, senior positions in the public service and parastatal organizations have been occupied by persons of different ethnic and racial groupings over the years. As a matter of fact, the first head of the public service and secretary to Cabinet was of Afrikaner origin. He was a leader of the public service for the whole of the first two decades of independence from 1967 to 1988.

c. The Botswana National Front (BNF)
Another form of political coalition worth noting in Botswana's experience was the formation of the Botswana National Front (BNF) in 1966. The BNF was formed out of faction from the BPP breakup which remained with the BPP President, Kgalemang Motsete. The grand goal of the BNF was to bring together patriotic forces and nationalists across the political spectrum into a political force in order to challenge the dominant BDP. The BNF, like BPP, was on the left of the political spectrum and was more ideologically aligned to socialist tendencies than the BPP. However, like the BPP, the BNF never managed to make significant impact across the country until about three decades later in the 1990s. The reasons for

the poor showing came from the same direction as the BPP. First, like the BPP but unlike the BDP, the BNF had a difficult time recruiting the leadership of the ruling families of the different ethnic groups and racial groupings. The second reason – which is not unrelated to the first – was its rather radical political leanings in the direction of socialism. Indeed, the Front had to bend over backward, ideologically, in 1967 to successfully recruit the disgruntled Chief Bathoen II of Bangwaketse to resign his chieftaincy to join them. Chief Bathoen II was a conservative traditionalist who opposed the BDP government for taking away the powers of the chiefs, thereby marginalising them.

The recruitment of Chief Bathoen II was a significant positive step by the BNF. Bathoen won the first seat for the party in Parliament in the 1969 election when all the three seats in his chiefdom elected the BNF candidates including himself and, even more significantly, defeated the then Vice President, Masire, and the then BDP Secretary-General. Mr Masire had to be brought back to parliament under the specially elected member ticket. Although the BNF appealed to a section of the labour movement and subsequently to the youth and urban voters, the BNF's political coalition had only a limited impact. Most of the anticipated in-roads into the BDP support in rural areas did not happen. As with the rest of the opposition parties, the success of the BNF has been further hampered by both the lack of resources and internal disagreements which saw the party break into a several smaller factions/parties during the 1990s.

In recent years, efforts have been made by different opposition parties to form broader coalitions. For instance, in the 2004 election the BNF, BPP and Botswana Alliance Movement (BAM – itself a formation of three smaller opposition parties) formed an electoral pact which however did not make any impact on their overall support. For the 2009 election, the BAM has gone into an electoral pact with the Botswana Congress Party (BCP is a faction of BNF) and the New Democratic Front (NDF – latest faction of the BNF). The impact of this new coalition on the electorate remains to be seen.

d. The All-Party Conference as a Grand Coalition
The Botswana leadership has been ingenious in the way it has handled political challenges and disagreement. In the previous section, we referred to former President Mogae's strategy of resolving the issues of perceived discrimination and under-representation in the House of Chiefs by certain minority groups. Mr. Mogae addressed this challenge by setting up a consultative commission to solicit ideas. The Commission served several positive objectives as it went around the country addressing both the majority and minority groups. First, it raised for debate the concerns of the minority groups. Secondly, through the debates in the *Kgotla*, it prepared the nation for change by deliberating on what were significant national unity issues. And thirdly, it generated ideas about how to

solve the issues amicably in the national interest. Similarly during the late 1990s when for the first time the BDP felt the threat of opposition parties eroding its support, the ruling party established an All-Party Consultative Conference. The Conference was to discuss and build consensus on major political issues relating to electoral reform, the voting age and postal voting from outside the country. The opposition parties had been mobilising around these issues for some time and they were clearly gaining support about them.

Following a number of discussions at the Conference, a consensus was built to: (i) create an autonomous electoral body run by an Independent Electoral Commission; (ii) lower the voting age from 21 to 18; (iii) allow for postal voting; and (iv) set the limit to the term of Office of the President at two terms of five years each. These reforms were then taken through parliament and translated into law. The value of the Conference was its inclusiveness and consensus building. It included political parties which would not have had the opportunity to express their views if the issue had simply gone straight to parliament because they were not represented there. Secondly, it gave an opportunity to the ruling party to save face as it looked less like a victory for the opposition parties. The All Party Conference has declined in importance and now meets less frequently. This is largely because the opposition parties have become weak and voters' confidence in them significantly reduced. Nevertheless the Conference remains in existence as an informal consultative structure on political consensus building.

Traditional and Modern Leadership Coalition

Different scholars have celebrated Botswana's ability to graft the traditional and modern institutions in a manner that made them work towards common goals of nation-building and development. Indeed, the institutions of chieftaincy and of the *Kgotla* (traditional assembly place and court) which were political, judicial and social pillars of the pre-colonial and colonial Tswana society still exist in a robust form as parts of the modern democratic Botswana. The chiefs, for instance, are part of the parliament through the advisory House of Chiefs. They are also an integral part of the judicial and administrative systems at local and national levels (Interviews with Goboletswe Ketsitlile on 29 December 2008; Tebelelo Seretse on 9 January 2009; Botsweletse Kingsley Sebele on 10 January 2009). In fact, contrary to the view of some writers on this subject, their role is not just limited to local government from where their power derives. They are national leaders in that they conduct judicial appeal cases and are also custodians of culture and tradition across the country. This notwithstanding, some young chiefs are increasingly being enticed into joining partisan politics and prefer to directly represent their tribal/geographical areas of their traditional authority in parliament in the same manner as Chief Bathoen II did in the 1960s and 1970s.

The *Kgotla* too has remained a central forum in the life of Botswana's democracy. All key decisions on policy, law and development have to be tabled at each main *Kgotla* for both debate and information. The *Kgotla* is also the place where the majority of the population still goes for redress or relief of any injustice or disputes with each other. The *Kgotla* also serves as the institution where marriage is consummated or dissolved. Many citizens go to the *Kgotla* to conclude or dissolve their marriages and pay the still highly recognized system of *lobola* – bride price (Interview with Tebelelo Seretse on 9 January 2009).

How did the leaders manage to successfully blend the country's traditional and modern institutions? This is an important question given that many African countries decided to abolish traditional institutions after independence. The cases of Mozambique where the new government abolished traditional institutions, or Uganda, Lesotho and Ghana where traditional institutions became either too powerful or became a stubborn opposition to the success of the modern state are just a few of the many cases in the continent. Swaziland, for instance, has chosen to make the new institutions subservient to the traditional ones and this has not worked well either as the country has become divided and conflict ridden. So, the fact that Botswana seems to have succeeded in peacefully blending traditional and modern institutions should be regarded as a subject of significant achievement on the part of the country's leaders and elites.

This process of blending was neither easy nor smooth. It involved several struggles, resistance, resignation and a carefully designed political strategy of coalition building and inclusiveness by the new elite. Before independence, the chiefs were powerful individuals controlling land, natural resources, culture, tradition and the law and custom in their individual territories around the country. At the independence talks they were therefore determined to retain their powers. On the other hand, the new elites and the outgoing Protectorate Administration did not see the future in rule by chiefs. The new elite had been picked by the Protectorate Administration much earlier to participate in formative semi-political bodies such as the African Advisory Council, the Joint Advisory Council and, ultimately, the Legislative Council which gave rise to the independence Constitutional Talks in the early 1960s.

As we noted earlier, the new political elite could be divided into two groups – a minority of radicals and a majority of ideological moderates. However, both groups were convinced that chiefly rule was undemocratic and had to be replaced by a national democratic government. They were all therefore determined to exclude the chiefs from active politics (Masire, 2006).

The leaders wanted to establish a judicious selection and integration of some strategic traditional institutions to articulate them with modern democratic institutions so as to indigenise the country's democratic tradition. In this section the institution-building skills of the leaders and elites of Botswana are demonstrable.

The leaders were clear on the agenda for change, but also recognized the importance of buying time, when appropriate, and acting decisively when necessary. We focus particularly on the strategies that were used to curtail the powers of the chiefs and establish new and more representative institutions, such as the land boards, district councils and the new structure of tribal administration. These new more democratic institutions were built on the chiefs' power and authority, while at the same time carving a new role for the chiefs themselves (Interviews with Goboletswe Ketsitlile on 29 December 2008; Tebelelo Seretse on 9 January 2009; Botsweletse Kingsley Sebele on 10 January 2009; Patrick Molutsi on 22 February 2009). What leadership skills and strategies did the new elite use to build this articulation which elsewhere in Africa has not worked?

The chiefs did not take kindly to the major changes and curtailment of their powers. Since 1966 conflicts and contestations have come to characterize the relationships between modern leaders and their institutions and the traditional leaders and their institutions. These relationships involved protest and confrontation where some of the chiefs who were not happy with the new arrangement, particularly the curtailment of their powers such as Chief Bathoen II decided to leave chieftaincy for active politics. Chief Bathoen II resigned in 1969, and joined the opposition Botswana National Front (BNF). He later challenged Ketumile Masire, Botswana's Vice President at the time, and defeated him in the 1969 elections. He was in parliament from 1969 through 1986 when he resigned. He was later appointed President of the Customary Court of Appeal. Even then, those chiefs who openly protested were few in number. This showed that the curtailment of the powers of the chiefs was skilfully managed by the new leaders and elite.

Where appropriate the state used a 'carrot and stick approach to bring chiefs under control and discipline. Several chiefs such as Neale Sechele of Bakwena, Seepapitso IV of Bangwaketse and Besele Montshioa of Barolong, were all suspended from their duties at different times for what was considered indiscipline and misbehaviour, often against politicians and local public officers. The transformation of chiefs into salaried public servants also meant that they lost all the rights to collect levies from their people. The most recent confrontation was in 2007 when the Government introduced a Bill that introduced a mandatory retirement age for chiefs at 70 years. Another successful strategy was management by neutralisation whereby several new non-chiefs were appointed into the chieftaincy both at the local level and to the House of Chiefs. This served to neutralise and weaken the voices of the stronger chiefs. Such appointees included former public officers such as Gontse, previously the Clerk of Parliament, Maforaga – former District Commissioner – was appointed Chief in Palapye; and the former Member of Parliament for Kgatleng, Mr Greek Ruele, was made chief of Artesia.

The leaders also used incorporation and integration to manage chiefs. Chiefs were involved in local councils and land boards, the establishment of new traditional institutions such as the Traditional Court of Appeal to which Bathoen was appointed, then Lichwe II and also Chief Monare Gaborone of Batlokwa. Such institutions did not only present opportunities to disgruntled chiefs but also helped to integrate them as part of the new ruling coalition. In the process, the traditional institutions and leaders were skilfully moulded to become an integral part of the modern state and its democratic institutions in dispensing justice, public consultation, gender and ethnic involvement as well as promotion of the cultural identity of Botswana.

However, the part that remains unresolved and poses a potential source of tension and conflict is the straddling of chieftaincy and political office by some chiefs. This is the situation where the chief becomes a politician or senior public officer without resigning his or her chieftaincy position. Since chiefs are supposed to be non-partisan and neutral leaders above politics, the situation first allowed by the ruling party to co-opt the current President as a politician and Member of Parliament while still remaining a Chief of Bangwato has established a precedent which has already been envied by the other young chiefs.

Taken together, all measures described above reduced the chiefs' powers and made it possible for the post-colonial state to manage and govern the country without compromising state capacity to rule and define the overall democratic politics. Despite reforms and changes, chiefs remain popular in the areas they preside over. Even then, a key lesson can be drawn from this. A careful management of traditional chiefs and their institutions whereby they have been given some recognition, accommodated and thus integrated into the new state, does not only ensure stability but also ensures that they continue to play a meaningful role – however small – in development programmes. And this has also safeguarded Botswana's political identity and its subsequent post-colonial development.

Centralising Key Resources in the Hands of the National as Opposed to the Local State

The success of the new state depended on its ability to bring key natural resources under its control. Since most of these were in the hands of chiefs, private individuals and (in the case of freehold land) in the hands of white settler farmers, getting these resources peacefully transferred from the original owners to the central government was yet another demonstration of skilful leadership and respect for human rights of those affected. In this section we focus of three types of resources: land – both tribal and freehold; mineral resources; and wildlife resources.

At independence the country's land tenure stood as 48% tribal land, 47% Crown Land and the remaining 5% was freehold land. There were several challenges involved with this land tenure and its distribution. In the tribal areas, there was shortage of land in some and in others it was under-utilised and poorly managed. The tribal land was for tribesmen and restricted to those citizens crowded in small tribal areas. The freehold owners also underutilised their land and some were absentee landlords (Mazonde, 1987).

The transfer of land ownership and control from the tribe to the central state and from freehold white settler owners was not an easy process for the new leadership of Botswana. The new state, however, was clear that land was a key resource which needed to be released from the control of the chiefs and private individuals in order to be given to citizens to develop and improve the country's agriculture and, where possible, for government to utilise for other purposes such as mining and wildlife development and management. The policies and programmes of the ruling Botswana Democratic Party, which overwhelmingly won the first democratic elections in 1965, identified agriculture and therefore the land question as key to the success of the economy. The thrust of the government's policy on land was first to:

- Change the control and ownership of the communal land to individuals to either freehold ownership or leasehold;
- Promote large individual ownership in order to encourage productivity and better conservation practices.
- Acquire through purchase freehold land from white settlers and give it back to communities where there was land shortage.
-

a. Managing Tribal Land

The first steps in all this were to introduce legislation that changed the chiefs' custodianship and allowed government to buy land from freehold owners.

With regard to tribal land, two major land policies were initiated in the first decade of independence. The Tribal Land Act of 1968 and the Tribal Grazing Land Policy of 1975 both succeeded in taking/reducing the chiefs' control of tribal land and establishing individual control of large ranches of tribal land.

The first piece of legislation created a new organization – the land board, as the custodian of tribal land allocation, administration and recipient of any revenue generated from such land by its private users. The second piece of legislation sought to achieve three principles of policy: increased production and job creation; better conservation management; and social justice – reservation of land for the next generations. These legislations were bold steps by the new elite and the leadership of the new state. The policies were controversial and in many ways tested the power and control of the chiefs over their subjects. The chiefs strongly opposed both pieces of legislation but they were skilfully managed and, in the end, they became part of the ownership of these land reforms.

This study shows that these Acts contributed to Chief Bathoen II resigning his post as chief of Bangweketse in 1969 and joining opposition politics. Other vocal chiefs were either incorporated into new state functions such as the appointment of Chief Linchwe II of Bakgatla as the Botswana Ambassador to the United States in 1969 or they were advised to co-operate or resign. Clearly the new leaders here used incorporation and inclusion as a means of building a coalition for policy consensus. However, where this was difficult the leaders were willing to use threats of exclusion to ensure success of policy. Masire (2006) provides elaborate evidence of this other part of the state strategy.

The success of land policies however, derived more from the broader elite coalition base which supported them. Many of the elite identified with reforms and became important local champions of these reforms. The establishment of new local government institutions – tribal administration, local councils, land boards and the new pattern of district administration – were major institutional innovations which both intended and successfully served to diminish the powers of the chiefs and brought representative politics into operation at local level. The creation of these new institutions involved much conflict, accommodation and coalition of elites who worked together in the national interest. The main losers were the chiefs who were given a role in Parliament – in the House of Chiefs – and also the opportunity to chair the first district councils and land boards, but were gradually replaced. New traditional judicial structures – such as the Customary Court of Appeal – further created opportunities for chiefs to find a new role away from the developmental agenda of the local councils.

The new political stage opened with major democratic reforms that directly curtailed the power and authority of the chiefs on such matters as administration of land, planning and execution of development programmes and general responsibility for law and order in their areas of operation. Such reforms were captured in the establishment of elected local councils in 1965 and land boards in 1970. Effectively, the legislation on chieftaincy, local councils and tribal land of 1965, 1966 and 1967 respectively resulted in the end of the traditional leadership of the past and consequently opened a new chapter driven by conflict, coercion and reluctant co-operation between the new state and the chiefs (Interviews with Tebelelo Seretse on 9 January 2009; Botsweletse Kingsley Sebele on 10 January 2009; Kentse Rammidi on 5 February 2009).

The reforms gave rise to four new or re-structured local institutions – district/town councils, land boards, district administration (representing central government at local level) and the chiefs' own tribal administration. The local councils, land boards and district administration all re-shaped and confined the powers of the chiefs to leadership only in customary and traditional justice areas. The *Kgotla* – the tribal court and a ceremonial place for debates and other important events in the community – became the new consultative forum for national leaders. Ministers, Members of Parliament, Councillors and public servants all used the *Kgotla* to consult with the people in their constituencies to gather ideas and explain government policies and programmes. In this way, the *Kgotla* remains a major site for policy formulation and a forum that is used to build consensus around major ideas and policies. The chiefs on the other hand use the *Kgotla* more to conduct court hearings and settlement of disputes. This is a remarkable illustration of a *hybrid institutional arrangement*, serving and incorporating both 'customary' and 'modern' political and social functions. Moreover, it illustrates the virtue of indigenous institutional formation which is both appropriate and locally legitimate.

b. Re-Tribalising Freehold Land

Around some towns and in some tribal areas land was very scarce. Yet, around other towns like Lobatse, Gaborone and Francistown, prime land was privately owned by individuals and companies, mainly of European origin. The government chose to deal with the challenges of shortage of urban land and in some tribal areas through negotiated purchase of land from private owners. This process started way back in the immediate years of independence and has continued up until the present period. Farms have been purchased and handed over to communities in Northeast District, Batlokwa and Balete and Barolong areas. The process has been smooth though expensive for the government.

c. Introducing New Wildlife Management Regime

The Crown Land which constituted 47% of the total land area was transformed into State Land and thereby became the property of the Central Government. However, in many places in the Kalahari and elsewhere, Crown Land had been effectively used as tribal land where communities raised animals, produced crops and collected different types of wildlife. The new government took steps to transform most of this land into game reserves and national parks. It introduced new restrictive regimes against which local communities reacted strongly. Hunting for instance, was regulated and rationed. Only people of San origin were initially permitted to hunt throughout the year but they too were subsequently restricted. The case of Central Kalahari Game Reserve (CKGR), where the San people have taken Government to court several times and often won the cases, typifies the democratic process with which the wildlife reforms were as important as the changes in the tribal and freehold land tenures.

In many areas surrounding National Parks and Game Reserves communities were always pitted against Central Government. There were two reasons for this. First, they wanted to access the wildlife resources without restrictions as before. This could not be allowed and they were often caught and fined by Game Scouts. In the second instance, wildlife animals crossed into their areas and destroyed both their crops and killed their animals. These issues have caused persistent conflict and disagreement between the Central Government and the communities next to the national wildlife resources. This has required a lot of management skills from local and national leaders.

d. Acquiring Mineral Rights

Faced with limited resources at independence, the political elite not only took a proactive role in development, but they also carefully entered into a strategic alliance with international capital regarding the ownership and management of mineral resources. The state established both control of mineral rights and a strategic partnership. This partnership has been described, by some of our respondents, as one of the best to be entered between a multi-national company and a government of a developing country (Interviews with Botsweletse Kingsley Sebele on 10 January 2009; Kentse Rammidi on 5 February 2009; Lt Gen. Mompati Merafhe on 9 March 2009). As a result of this, minerals have not only been the pillar of Botswana's economy but they have generally been used for the benefit of all. The situation contrast sharply with a number of countries in Africa where they became a source of destabilisation, conflict and misery.

The new elites that assumed office at independence, particularly under the leadership of Seretse Khama, played a crucial role in ensuring that mineral rights were ceded from the different ethnic groupings to the central government, following an extended consultation process with the different ethnic groups. This was made easy because the first minerals were discovered in the Bangwato area, the birthplace of Seretse Khama. The minerals discovered were copper and nickel in Selibe Phikwe, and later diamonds in Orapa-Letlhakane which was also in the Bangwato area. Ceding mineral rights to the Central Government started there. As a result, the rest of the tribes had no problem with this arrangement. Even then, Chief Bathoen II was against the ceding of mineral rights but he gave in following skilful negotiations with the leaders (Interviews with Botsweletse Kingsley Sebele on 10 January 2009; Lt Gen. Mompati Merafhe on 9 March 2009). Since then, large diamond deposits have been discovered in the area of Bangwaketse of former Chief Bathoen II.

More importantly, there was a consensus amongst the leadership that minerals were a strategic resource. As a result, they used their skills to enter into a strategic partnership with international capital. De Beers, in particular, became a critical partner forming a uniquely successful coalition that mined and managed sales and shared mineral revenues in such a way that it has benefited the country's development programme in a sustainable way.

Governing Coalitions – The Modern Democratic State in Practice

Botswana has been a stable unitary state since independence. How did the elites develop and manage to break the physical and socio-cultural, ethnic and racial barriers? What factors in terms of material and social conditions helped them form successful coalitions that contributed to the formation and success of Botswana as a 'developmental state'? This section explains the historical origins of the modern elites and their background in terms of education, ideological orientation, racial and ethnic accommodation and economic survival strategies. It also looks at the external threats that helped to mould the new coalitions into a common purpose. The strategies adopted to create an open society accommodating different groups and foreigners were central to the success of the country's politics and economy up to date.

a. The Making of the Modern Elite

The modern elite in Botswana had its provenance and was formed in the second decade of the twentieth century. The writings of missionaries and early travellers such as Robert Moffat, John Mackenzie and David Livingstone in the eighteenth and nineteenth centuries show that the points of call and centres of power in many Tswana communities were chiefs – the traditional elites. The western educated elites did not appear until the 1920s and 1930s following the attainment of some western missionary-led education. Such education was for the first and second generations (defined for the purposes of this paper as the periods from 1920-1950 and from 1950-1970 respectively) and was received largely outside the country. A few citizens, disproportionately from royal families (Parsons, Henderson and Tlou, 1995), managed with the assistance of missionaries to go through secondary and tertiary education in South Africa and what was then Southern Rhodesia (now Zimbabwe).

By the mid-1940s Botswana had developed a small but identifiable first generation of a new elite. This, as we saw earlier, was a group that contested state power with the traditional leadership. In the case of Botswana, the new elite had been forming since the 1920s and 1930s compared to other neighbouring countries where the provision of western-Christian education enabled the new elite to form earlier in the late nineteenth century (Molutsi, 1989, Parsons, 1993). The new elite were socially different in values, ethics, education and political aspirations from the traditional leaders. Sections of this elite, operating at local level of individual Native Reserves/Chiefdoms, started challenging chieftaincy rule in the 1930s (Schapera 1955, 1970 and 1994; Molutsi, 1989). Individual names such as the Ratshosas in Bangwato territory, Masire and others in the Bangwaketse territory, and Dr. Molema in the Barolong territory, come to mind in terms of their vociferous criticisms of the chiefs' rule. The emergence and local presence of the new elite could not escape the attention of the colonial administration which began to use them as alternate leaders, either to support the administration's local development initiatives or purposely to moderate the chiefs' occasional autocratic tendencies (Molutsi, 1989, Parsons, Henderson and Tlou, 1995, Masire, 2006; Interviews with Gobe Matenge on 19 December 2008; Patrick Molutsi on 22 February 2009).

As alternative leaders to the traditional leaders, the new elite came to the fore in the 1950s when the hitherto separate African and European Advisory Councils were merged to form the Joint Advisory Council. Not only were the chiefs and leaders of the white settler communities appointed to the new Council, but educated non-chiefly individuals such as Quett Masire, Moutlakgolo Nwako and Goareng Mosinyi were also brought in. It was here too that the battle of values and contestation for the future leadership of the postcolonial state came to the fore. Indeed the political and cultural proximity between the colonial administrators, the European representatives and the new elite, on the one hand, and the traditional leaders, on the other, was demonstrated (Fawcus, 2000) during the constitutional talks in 1963.

The last of the colonial institutions, the Legislative Council formed in 1959, ushered in Botswana's independence in 1966 and showed a disproportionate representation in favour of the new elite as against the traditional leaders. It now became clearer than ever before that the people being mentored into the inheritance of the post-colonial state were not the chiefs and the wider traditional leadership but the new elite and their new political organizations. It was during the formation of political parties in the late 1950s and early 1960s that the battle for postcolonial state power between the chiefs and the new elite came to its peak and new alliances were formed and points of departure made.

Beginning in the late 1940s, the people of the Bechuanaland Protectorate began to experience a greater desire for education. A number of initiatives to establish educational institutions of higher learning were started. In the early 1930s, two such initiatives began in the North East and at Kgale around Gaborone (the modern capital of Botswana). The Tati Institution sought to promote the education of the Bakalanga community while the Forest Hill Agriculture School sought to bring students from different parts of the country. The real impact of education at secondary level came in the 1950s when new secondary schools were established by Catholics in Kgale as St. Joseph's College, Moeng College by the Bangwato tribe under their Chief Tshekedi Khama in Moeng and subsequently in the transfer of Tigerkloof under the new name Moeding College from South Africa to Otse in Botswana. These three organizations became premier secondary schools educating students from all parts of the country. It was from these schools that a small number of good performers subsequently proceeded to study at the new University of Botswana, Lesotho and Swaziland (UBLS) based in Lesotho (Interviews with Kesitegile Gobotswang on 15 January 2009; Festina Bakwena on 11 February 2009; Patrick Molutsi on 22 February 2009).

The majority of the elite were of Tswana-speaking background, coming from the country's main ethnic groups and speaking the same language and with common cultural background. The first generation of this small but very critical group had been educated largely outside the country in premier Christian African multi-discipline institutions in South Africa such as Lovedale, Tigerkloof and Fort Hare University in the Eastern Cape.

The review of secondary sources to date and interviews show that the elite coalition in Botswana was influenced by its educational background as well as by the geo-political challenges facing Botswana before and immediately after independence.

Masire's case study also shows how the emerging elite of former tribesmen – who came from very different parts of the country – were formed. This group of schoolmates had commonly studied together in South Africa. They came back to Botswana to work in the then limited number of schools as teachers, newspaper reporters, junior clerks and other junior administrators in the Protectorate Administration of the 1940s and 1950s. Masire also refers to his friends and members of his ethnic group such as Bias Mookodi, Archie Mogwe, Peter Mmusi but also mentions Goareng Mosinyi, Moutlakgola Nwako from outside the Bangwaketse, and a few others who with him came to lead the new independent state as politicians, diplomats, senior bureaucrats and political party leaders. Masire's book also illustrates a strong religious education and associated anti-communist ideology of the Southern Africa region of the 1940s and 1950s.

Another case study of the new elites and their differences from the traditional elites comes from none other than the first president of Botswana himself – the late Seretse Khama. Mr. Seretse Khama was the heir to the Bangwato crown, the biggest ethnic group in the country. His father Sekgoma Khama died during the early years of Seretse's childhood, and Seretse grew up under the guardianship of his uncle – his father's younger brother Tshekedi Khama. Seretse, like other Batswana children of his age and times, went to school in the local primary school, but for his secondary schooling he went to study outside the country. There he studied with several other students from Botswana in South Africa in the 1930s and 1940s. These were times when African nationalism was gaining momentum while the Soviet-led socialist ideology was slowly taking root in the African continent. In South Africa, the racial ideologies which had informed the Hertzog government of the 1920s to early 1930s were also taking a new turn as Prime Minister D.F. Malan and his group in the post War period prepared the design and implementation of "grand apartheid".

However, Seretse's specific experience came as a result of his studies in England from the mid-1940s, where he was exposed to liberal political ideologies and where he married a white lady from London. His marriage brought him and his wife harsh personal experiences that have been too well documented to warrant repetition here. However, his experience points to the impact that individual leader's experiences do sometimes have on the wider society and its development.

The first outcome of his bi-racial marriage was the division it brought to his own ethnic group. One group sided with him, while the other sided with his uncle, Tshekedi Khama. The long struggle that resulted ultimately led to reconciliation with his uncle, and Seretse's rejection of the tribal traditional leadership role for a broader national leadership role. So, for Seretse, it was not only racism and racist ideology to which he became exposed and which he rejected, but chieftaincy and its limited tribal base. As a consequence, Seretse Khama became a national hero and a unifying figure for the racial groupings in the country and the different ethnic/tribal leaders who were not chiefs at the time. The new conciliatory politics saw Seretse and his uncle Tshekedi Khama in 1959 participate in the preparations for independence when the British Protectorate Administration (which had been seriously implicated in the "Seretse's Marriage Affair") began to reach out to involve him in the different political and development committees.

During their studies, the new elite also met other people from countries of the Southern African region. Some of these schoolmates later became political party members back in Botswana. Typically, there was a number of South Africans (Xhosa, Zulu and Sotho speakers) fleeing the heightened racial conflict in their country in the late 1940s and 1950s and they too came to settle in Botswana and worked in schools and other administrative jobs. This group also ultimately formed an integral part of the new elite. Among these were key names such as Tsoebebe, Mdlauli, Ngcongco, Vanga, Mzondeki, Motsepe and others (see Parsons, Henderson and Tlou, 1995; Interviews with Peter Letlhogonolo Siele on 31 December 2008; Patrick Molutsi on 22 February 2009).

The second generation came from a similar socio-cultural and educational background as the first and evolved in the 1970s. They, and most of the subsequent generations, were largely driven into public service and teaching jobs. Compared to their predecessors, the second and third generations of elite were better educated and trained. They tended to study social sciences, humanities and education with only a few going for natural sciences. These two generations were therefore destined for public service leadership and much less for political leadership which in any case was still dominated by the first generation. Hence, many of the second and third generation elites became permanent secretaries, directors of different departments in government, school principals and headmasters as well as teachers, nurses and social workers.

The common feature was rapid social mobility to the higher echelons of the civil service and therefore to positions of strategic leadership in public sector policy formation and implementation. Because they were relatively more educated and trained than their predecessors, the second and third generations enjoyed some relative autonomy from the politicians who allowed them a lot of space to initiate policy and play a professional advisory role to the politicians (See Wiseman, 1977; Wallis, 1989; Holm, 1989; Egner and Grant, 1989; Somolekae, 1993; Tordoff, 1997; Samatar, 1999; Acemoglu, Johnson and Robinson, 2001). Internal elite cohesion among the bureaucrats was quite high. Early tensions which had been related to racial differences were successfully resolved (Republic of Botswana, 1966; Molutsi, 1983). This demonstrates the value of education in the processes of elite formation and coalition-building.

Economic Viability of the State at Independence

Botswana's independence in 1966 coincided with one of the country's occasional severe droughts. The country was poor in every sense, with no clear source of income. The agricultural sector, which had since the 1930s been seen as the only real potential economic activity of substance was going through a difficult time which also demonstrated the sector's vulnerability. Under the circumstances, the new leaders looked to the departing British government to provide a temporary economic package in the form of budget subsidy. This strategy and the recognition of the poverty that cut across the population seems to have been critical in the evolution of the *culture of economic prudence* that has become one of the pillars of the country's economic planning and development discourse (Interviews with Botsweletse Kingsley Sebele on 10 January 2009; Leach Tlhomelang on 3 February 2009; Festina Bakwena on 11 February 2009; Lt Gen. Mompati Merafhe on 9 March 2009). The culture of scarcity and the challenge of creating a viable state later manifested itself in the ideological orientation that emphasized *self-reliance (ipelegeng, national unity)* and *economic independence.*

The leadership stressed *national unity* and *social harmony (kagisanyo)* as the unifying factors that would allow the country to focus on development and achieve the goals of economic independence and political stability. The findings of our research show that it was *the challenge of creating a viable independent state that provided an objective rallying point for leaders and elite coalitions in Botswana.* The material circumstances of the country and the implications of this for its success as an independent state were crucial in promoting a momentum for the formation of a grand elite coalition at political, public service and economic development levels. In particular, the introduction and entrenchment of the culture of a five-yearly development planning process that engaged local and central government, private and public sectors, civil society and religious leaders and elites in an elaborate process of priority selection of projects and development agenda-setting, has been a critical factor and process helping to build and sustain developmental coalitions in Botswana.

The Evolution of the National Development Planning Process

Botswana's development programme has since independence been underpinned by the five-to-six year rolling plans called the National Development Plan. In 2009, the country will begin its tenth such Plan. The first plan was formulated in 1963 and was called a Transitional Development Plan. Since then every five to six years the country has undergone an extensive process of project selection, prioritisation and resource allocation. Several points and questions need to be discussed here concerning the planning process. Is it truly consultative? Does it make a difference? Who are the real drivers, and who benefits?

The Botswana's planning process and its product – the National Development Plan – has been questioned by some scholars as well as celebrated by others as showing both the quality of leadership and the country's genuine commitment to a democratic decision-making process. The planning process involves a number of discrete steps. First, the lead ministry – namely the Ministry of Finance and Development Planning (MFDP) – normally starts the process by producing what they call a Key Issues Paper (KIP). This is a general framework which states possible issues to be focussed on during the coming plan. The KIP is determined by a number of factors. The first is the continuing agenda from the prior and just-ending plan. Second, are the new challenges to the country's development; and third are new opportunities and possibilities. For example, while poverty alleviation, the social development agenda – education, health, water and agriculture and infrastructure development – have remained permanent priorities and stable in each plan, HIV/AIDS, crime prevention, anticorruption and others have been emerging issues in the past two development plans. On the basis of KIP, each sectoral ministry and department – including local government institutions – are given the opportunity to both comment on, and develop, their Sectoral Key Issues Papers (SKIPs).

On the basis of KIP and SKIPs, the MFDP then produces yet another framework called – Macroeconomic Strategy Paper – which defines total estimated cost allocation proposals for each ministry and sector. For example, the Macroeconomic Strategy Paper might state that the total estimated cost of the Development Plan 7 is P250 billion (total is for five years) of which P50 billion will go to education. The next step will be for each ministry and its broad stakeholders at central and local levels, also including and both public and private interests, to work together to prioritise which programmes and projects will go into the plan. In this example, the Ministry of Education and Skills Development would prioritise in terms of which schools and other facilities are to be built and for how much. From the individual sectoral consultations, draft chapters for the next plan would be done. These would then be compiled into the draft plan which goes to the National Consultative Forum to discuss and modify. The forum then has the opportunity to question, change and add new programmes and projects across sectors. It is after this third stage that the draft plan goes to Parliament for debate and final approval.

The planning process is designed to involve the lowest structures at the local level called village development committees (VDCs) through to District Development Committees (DDC) to the National Development Conference (Forum). The political structures from district councils, Cabinet/Executive up to Parliament are involved at each stage (Interviews with Festina Bakwena on 11 February 2009; Lt Gen. Mompati Merafhe on 9 March 2009). In this way, the elites at all levels are mobilised to focus on the plan and make decisions about the priorities for their part of the country. Certainly, the Plan is a gate-keeping tool and the players have come to realise this. If your project – school or clinic – is in the Plan then you are happy and would expect it to be built during the plan period. If, however, your project is left out then you know *a priori* that it would not be done in the current plan period. In short, the plan is a bargaining tool, an interactive political process between the different local and central government elites, public, private sector and non-governmental elites. They each bargain to come up with something to serve their needs (Interviews with Festina Bakwena on 11 February 2009; Patrick Molutsi on 22 February 2009; Lt Gen. Mompati Merafhe on 9 March 2009).

From the foregoing description, it can be seen that the planning process and the National Development Plan in Botswana symbolises a grand coalition of elites at work. It is here that voices are heard and bargains and balancing of interests are made.

The Material Base of the Elite

The fundamental characteristic of the Botswana leaders and elites, especially the first generation, was that they were socially and economically tied to the agricultural economy where the majority of the population lived and eked out a living. The question might therefore be asked as to what made them an 'elite'? The answer is simply that although they were trained in western education which influenced their value system, behavioural patterns and sub-cultures and therefore made them different from the rest of the society, they essentially depended on agriculture for a living. They were, on one hand agents of change and advocates of an alternative system of governance to that of the chiefs' rule – traditional governance institutions; while, and on the other hand, they were farmers. Materially, the new elite depended like everyone else on ownership of livestock – cattle predominantly – and the production of crops for their own consumption and commercial sale. This situation made the elite highly dependent on the agricultural economic base, hence our description of it as an "agrarian elite".

How did the material base of this elite influence the policies and programmes of the new state? Did their economic interests influence state policies and programmes? If so, did these policies and programmes benefit only the elite as an interest group or did such policies and programmes also benefit the wider society?

This section uses the land question and policies on agriculture and livestock as measures of how the leadership and the ruling elite built coalitions and patterns of consensus that were critical for state formation and the stability of the economy in the early years of independence. Although the elite has remained strongly linked to the agrarian sector, the section shows that their growth in size and diversification in interest has led to subsequent generations of the elite focusing on the urban economy – private sector, estate agent and property development as areas of investment and material dependence away from agriculture. Formal employment has also absorbed the focus of a large proportion of the succeeding generations of elites and thereby substantially reduced their reliance on the agrarian sector.

Strategic Alliances with International Capital and Business

Many developing states depend a lot on the support and co-operation of bilateral aid, multi-lateral organizations/institutions and foreign direct investment (FDI) for their development success. In cases where the state has been hostile to external partners, the evidence shows a poor record of development performance at home. In Southern Africa, countries which were devastated by civil wars such as Mozambique, South Africa, Angola, Namibia and currently DRC have derived a lot of assistance and support from the international community simply because they have opened up to the external world. On the other hand Zimbabwe's recent experience is a typical case of difficult international relations which have deprived that country of much needed foreign assistance and investment.

Botswana's leaders and elite from the start based their development model on a free market economic strategy. Different types of external elites – donors, international organizations, foreign technical experts and foreign businesses and workers – have featured prominently in the development process of the country. This section unpacks the different types of foreign elites and their role in co-operating with Botswana's leadership to drive the country's development agenda. It shows that the orientation has been and remains that of accommodation rather than exclusion. Botswana has realised its success with the joint effort and co-operation of external interests in the private sector. The private sector in the mineral sector, in particular, carved out a strategic and enduring relationship with the Botswana state from very early on. Such relationship is epitomised in the ownership and sharing of the diamond revenues. This research has shown that the relationship between the state and the private sector in Botswana has been uniquely friendly, yet has crucially avoided collusion, rent-seeking or predatory behaviours.

a. The Mineral Coalition

The skills of Botswana's leadership are often said to have been displayed most vividly in the manner in which it formed and sustained an enduring coalition with mineral exploiting foreign companies. As new and reconciled leader of the Bangwato tribe, Tshekedi Khama and Seretse Khama had entered into a relationship with the Roan Selection Trust (RST) to exploit copper and nickel in Selibe Phikwe in the mid 1960s. This relationship was to endure into the post-independence period resulting in the formation of a new jointly owned company called Bangwato Corporation Limited (BCL) which still today mines copper and nickel in Selibe Phikwe in Botswana.

However, it is the diamond mining sector which has attracted international attention as an exemplary case of a harmonious and mutually beneficial relationship between a developing country and a powerful multinational company. When large diamond pipes were discovered in the mid-1960s, again in the Bangwato territory of Orapa and Letlhakane, the Government entered into a uniquely successful partnership with the De Beers Diamond Mining Company. De Beers which had for many years been mining diamonds in South Africa, Namibia and Angola – among other countries in the region – accepted a uniquely generous agreement with the government of Botswana whereby the Government and de Beers agreed to a 50/50 split of the diamond mining revenues. According to secondary sources and our current respondents, this was a highly favourable agreement to Botswana as in reality the government gained more through tax revenues from De Beers (Interviews with Botsweletse Kingsley Sebele on 10 January 2009; Patrick Molutsi on 22 February 2009; Lt Gen. Mompati Merafhe on 9 March 2009).

The careful negotiation skills of the Botswana leadership was again demonstrated in the late 1970s when yet another even larger and more valuable diamond Kimberlite pipe was discovered in Jwaneng in Bangwaketse territory in the south of Botswana. Here, the negotiations resulted favourably in the Government settling for sixty (60%) per cent of the revenue from the mine. Subsequently, a jointly owned company, named the De Beers–Botswana Mining Company (or DEBSWANA), was formed with equal membership and a chairmanship of the board rotating between officials from the Government of Botswana and De Beers. Today it is DEBSWANA which runs the diamond mines in Botswana. It is in this company that senior civil servants have taken turns to sit both on the DEBSWANA Board on behalf of Government and also some of them have been Executive directors of the DEBSWANA.

Among many such influential players was Mr. Festus Mogae who started off at DEBSWANA Board as the then Permanent Secretary in the Ministry of Finance and Development Planning (MFDP) in the 1980s. When he became the Minister in the same Ministry in the early 1990s his successor as Permanent Secretary of the same Ministry, Mr. Baledzi Gaolatlhe (now Minister of Finance and Development Planning), also became an influential member of the DEBSWANA Board. In fact, at one point in the late 1990s Mr. Gaolatlhe was the Managing Director of DEBSWANA for about two years. He left the post to become the Governor of the Central Bank until he joined politics and became the Minister of Finance and Development Planning in 1999 when Mr. Mogae became the President of Botswana. Besides Messrs Mogae and Gaolatlhe, the other prominent figure in the managing of DEBSWANA over the many years was Mr. Nchindo. He was the longest serving member of the board of DEBS-WANA and the company's Managing Director for many years.

Since the representation of both Government and De Beers in the DEBS-WANA Board was fifty–fifty, several other senior government officers were involved in the running of this long lasting coalition. Senior officers from the Ministry of Mineral Resources and Water Affairs and from the Office of the President became members of the Board of DEBSWANA. Indeed, the current Managing Director of DEBSWANA, since the retirement of Mr. Nchindo in 2004, Mr. Blackie Marole, gained his knowledge and experience of the diamond mining sector during his years as the Permanent Secretary in the Ministry of Mineral Resources and Water Affairs. The current Permanent Secretary to the President, who is also Secretary to Cabinet, Mr. Molale, is the current chairman of DEBSWANA. He is occupying this position as the government representative and he will in a few years pass the chairmanship to the De Beers representative on the Board.

At individual interest level, De Beers still has its own separate Office in Botswana which oversees the company's interest and ensures that it is adequately informed of government policies and other developments. It is interesting that in around 2005, De Beers appointed, for the first time, a female citizen, married to the Khama family, as its local Executive Director. This was interesting for two reasons.

First, it showed that trust had evolved between the two parties on the mining and sale of Botswana diamonds. De Beers must have felt that a citizen – of course with capability and experience – was appropriate at this time. Ms Sheila Khama has proved to be capable and a useful link between the De Beers and Government.

The second reason why the appointment of Ms Khama to the Executive Director position at De Beers at this time was interesting was that it came at a critical moment when the first twenty-five year contract between De Beers and the Government was expiring. The new contract had to be re-negotiated and it is clear that De Beers wanted to show that this relationship had not only benefited the country in terms of revenue sharing, but that citizens had been trained and developed to the highest level of skills in the diamond sector. Indeed, the other important role of this appointment was that Ms Khama brought with her extra social capital – her deep knowledge of the country and how it works – but more importantly her friendships, both formal and informal, with many officials on the government side. She had been a schoolmate at the University of Botswana with Mr. Molale, the Permanent Secretary to the President, and the current Managing Director of DEBSWANA, Mr. Blackie Marole. In addition, Sheila Khama has family ties with the current President, Mr. Ian Khama.

The timeliness of the appointment of Ms Sheila Khama becomes also important in the context of the negotiations of the substance of the second long term contract between the two parties. Since the mid-1980s the government side has been expressing concerns that De Beers was not doing enough to develop the downstream operations of diamond mining to the country. The operations of the diamond sorting subsidiary company – Botswana Diamond Valuing Company (BDVC) – were seen as insufficient for job creation and strategic placing of Botswana as one of the lead diamond producers around the world. The key issue then for the second longer term contract was going to be the need to bring diamond manufacturing operations from London and other parts of Europe and America, to Botswana. This was expected to help the Government effort to diversify the economy away from mineral dependency to other sectors. The beneficiation of diamonds will bring into the country more companies that buy and cut diamonds and thereby the jobs that accompany those processes.

Indeed, the Government's Mineral Advisory Committee, formed around the Ministry of Mineral Resources and Water Affairs, the Ministry of Finance and Development Planning, the Central Bank and the Office of the President, pressed hard for the Diamond Trading Company (DTC), the De Beers subsidiary based in London, to transfer its operations to Botswana as a requirement for the new contract with De Beers. This was a tall order for De Beers as DTC is a complex operation at the heart of the whole global marketing and sale of diamonds and it involves both high security and business intelligence of a political and economic nature. Moreover, other diamond producing countries in the region – South Africa, Namibia and Angola – were also negotiating on the same grounds in order to deepen diamond benefits to their economies.

However, De Beers finally conceded to the deepening of integrated diamonds operations in Botswana. It was agreed that DTC would ultimately transfer its operations from London to Gaborone and the related aggregation of diamonds from neighbouring countries as well as major sale of raw diamonds will now be done in Botswana. Since the signing of a favourable new long term contract between De Beers and the Government of Botswana in 2007, BDVC has been dissolved. A new building for DTC has been completed and some of DTC's operations have been transferred to Gaborone. Clearly, this time around, Botswana's leadership has demonstrated continuing skilful negotiations and leadership. While the contract must have been difficult for De Beers, the trust in Botswana government's intentions is not in doubt. In fact, until last year (2008), when Government sold some of its shares, the Government of Botswana owned up to 15% of shares in De Beers (Interview with Patrick Molutsi on 22 February 2009).

b. *The Public – Private Sector Coalition*

The political elite has also showed its commitment to attracting Foreign Direct Investment (FDI) not only by entering into partnerships with De Beers (as above), but it has also been working hard to create a conducive environment for the private sector. This was particularly urgent as there was a need to diversify the economy away from diamonds and to create new centres of wealth. Over the years government has done a lot to create a stable macroeconomic and political business environment to attract FDI. The company tax for instance is one of the lowest in the world, at 15% of profits, and the fiscal policies, exchange and prime lending interest rates have all been fine-tuned to support local and foreign private sector.

The government also introduced a number of business finance initiatives in the 1980s and 1990s to finance both local and foreign business development in the country. The Financial Assistance Policy (FAP) and its successor – the Citizen Entrepreneur Development Agency (CEDA) – have been intended to boost private investment in different sectors of the economy. However, several constraints in the public-private sector relationship which (at least according to the private sector) have been major stumbling blocks to its growth have been identified as bureaucratic red-tape, negative attitudes of public officers to private sector initiatives, high cost of utilities and the length of time it takes to assist businesses with critical services.

In response to these complaints, the government under President Masire's Administration established a high level consultative council (HLCC) in 1996, made up of high level representatives of government, private sector and labour (Land, 2002; Ntuane, 2007; Interviews with Gobe Matenge on 19 December 2008; Botsweletse Kingsley Sebele on 10 January 2009; Festina Bakwena on 11 February 2009). The HLCC has indeed since been entrenched as a very serious coalition of business-government interests, aimed at addressing economic development issues and finding solutions that are mutually beneficial. The HLCC meets twice a year and it is chaired by the President and all ministers, permanent secretaries attend on the government side, while the Botswana Chamber of Commerce and Industry and Manpower (BOCCIM) brings all their different sectoral members to this forum (Interviews with Gobe Matenge on 19 December 2008; Festina Bakwena on 11 February 2009; Patrick Molutsi on 22 February 2009). An even more effective element of the consultative process through the HLCC is the fact that sub-committees meet at sectoral levels (that is, education, commerce, finance, etc.) before they meet at a higher level. This has helped to bring public officers and private businesses much closer together in a constructive expression of state-business relations.

c. The Roles of Technical Assistance and Foreign Workers

The case of Botswana also shows that the donor community and international development organisations/agencies have also been liberally accepted and made part of the development partnership. They have thus played a crucial role in development, particularly in the early years of independence. Why? Was it necessitated by the challenges the country faced, especially economic threat and acute poverty as well as other factors?

It is important to note that – as in Japan at the end of the 19th century – there was also an inclination and willingness to accept foreign ideas and advice, where appropriate to the conditions of Botswana. In this respect, localisation was not rushed and introduced at the expense of merit. And in this way, expatriates played an important role in the economy by providing the much needed technical expertise (Parsons, Henderson and Tlou, 1995). As Masire (2006) noted, at the time one of the things that preoccupied them was the retention of an efficient administration that could deliver development programmes. This is also supported by the interviews we conducted (Interviews with Gobe Matenge on 19 December 2008; Botsweletse Kingsley Sebele on 10 January 2009; Festina Bakwena on 11 February 2009; Lt Gen. Mompati Merafhe on 9 March 2009).

There has also been a willingness by the leaders, elites and coalitions to use mineral wealth to introduce citizen empowerment initiatives also aimed at not only creating jobs but diversifying the economy as well. In this sense, there is no doubt that the government perceives the private sector as a partner in development.

Conclusion

This study has traced the origins of the modern developmental elite and state in Botswana. It has emphasized that politics and the process of managing politics do not alone determine political, bureaucratic, social and economic formations of a society. In the case of Botswana the elite has been analysed in terms of its ideological inclinations, political ideologies and their origins, and in terms of its governing and development strategies. Clearly, notwithstanding challenges which still remain, this study has shown that behind Botswana's political and economic success lies a genuinely conscious elite which has worked through consultation, consensus building and inclusive strategies to drive a successful developmental project.

Key elite coalitions and pacts formed across the traditional-modern divide, across political parties, across ethnic-racial cleavages, across the public and private sectors, and across employer and employee divisions, as well as state and non-state actors in business and non-governmental sectors were of critical importance. Leadership was also a vital factor in the successes of these elite coalitions. This study of the Botswana leaders, elites and coalitions suggest that the country achieved what it did out of carefully designed and managed strategies. The specific geo-political and ethno-historical *structural* contexts of the country at the time of independence and beyond were, and continue to be important factors. But they were not, on their own not enough in shaping the success of policy and strategy. Rather, what really made the difference was *agency,* that is the leaders' conscious effort to create particular type of politics and state that made Botswana into what it is today – a functioning democratic 'developmental state' – by establishing the political conditions and institutional arrangements for sustained growth and political stability.

This study also shows how a judicious balance between the various ethnic groups has ensured that no single group dominated the political space. Both at independence and up to the present time each group has continued to enjoy relative autonomy from each other and is able to enter political discourse as an identifiable group. For instance, political parties, parliament, executive membership of government and public service selections have tended to be inclusive of the different ethnic and racial groupings without reducing these mode of decision making into formal rules as they have unsuccessfully tried to do in some developing countries. Moreover, the judicious integration of traditional and modern elements also shows a conscious effort on the part of the leaders to build inclusive developmental coalitions. The mineral coalition that was crafted and the relative good use of the mineral proceeds for the benefit of all also demonstrate a commitment to change the lives of all, irrespective of their racial or ethnic origin.

Finally, the use of the National Development Plan in prioritising projects, its inclusive nature in the course of its production and the commitment to implement what is in the Plan shows skilful leadership and the drive to make a difference in the country. A combination of factors played a key role in the way in which leaders and elites in Botswana forged and sustained developmental coalitions to promote growth through institutional arrangements which were appropriate in the context of Botswana's history, and its collective national developmental aspirations

References

Acemoglu, D., S.Johnson, and J. Robinson, 2001, 'How Botswana Did It: Comparative Development in Sub-Saharan Africa', unpublished paper.

Bechuanaland Democratic Party, 1965, *Election Manifesto*, "This is What We Stand For", Serowe: Botswana Democratic Party.

Edge, W., 1998, 'Botswana: A developmental state', in Edge, W. and M. Lekorwe (eds), *Botswana Politics and Society.* Pretoria: Van Schaik.

Egner, B. & S. Grant, 1989, 'The private press and democracy', in Holm, J. & P. Molutsi (eds), *Democracy in Botswana.* Gaborone: Macmillan Botswana Publishing Company, pp 247-163.

Fawcus, P., 2000, *Botswana: the road to independence.* Gaborone: Pula Press.

Holm, J., 1989, 'How effective are interest groups in representing their members?' in Holm, J. & P. Molutsi (eds), *Democracy in Botswana.* Gaborone: Macmillan Botswana Publishing Company (Pty) Ltd.

Land, A., 2002, *Case Study on Structured Public-Private Sector Dialogue: The Experience from Botswana*, ACP Business Forum, Confederation of Zimbabwe Industries.

Leftwich, A., 1995, 'Bringing Politics Back', in 'Towards a Model of the Developmental State', *The Journal of Developmental Studies*, Vol. 31, No. 3, pp. 400–427.

Leftwich, A., 1996, *Democracy and Development.* Cambridge: Polity Press.

Masire, K., 2006, *Very brave or very foolish? Memoirs of an African Democrat* (edited by Stephen R. Lewis). Basingstroke: Palgrave Macmillan.

Maundeni, Z. 2001 'State Culture and the Botswana Developmental State', A Paper presented to the Department of Political and Administrative Studies, University of Botswana, 25 January.

Mazonde, I. N., 1987, 'The development of ranching and economic enterprise in eastern Botswana', PhD Thesis, University of Manchester.

Molutsi, P.P., 1983, 'Education and Development', paper presented at a Workshop of the Botswana Society, Gaborone.

Molutsi, P.P. 1989. 'The Ruling Class and Democracy in Botswana', in J. Holm, J & Molutsi, P (eds) *Democracy in Botswana.* Gaborone: Macmillan Botswana Publishing Company (Pty) Ltd.

Ntuane, B., 2007, Remarks by Hon. Botsalo Ntuane, Specially Elected Member of Parliament (Republic of Botswana) on the Legislators' Perspective of Public-Private Policy Dialogue in Botswana, GICC, Gaborone, 9 May, 2007.

Parsons N., W. Henderson and T. Tlou, 1995, *Seretse Khama: 1921–1980.* Gaborone: Botswana Society.

Parsons, Q.N., 1974, 'The economic history of Khama's country in Southern Africa', *Africa Social Research*, Lusaka: Vol.18.

—, 1985, 'The Evolution of Modern Botswana: Historical Revisions', in Picard, L. (ed.), *The Evolution of Modern Botswana.* London: Rex Collings.

—, 1993, *Seretse Khama as President of Botswana, 1966-1980: lessons for Southern African Democracy, non-racialism and unity?* Cape, ZA: University of Cape Town Press.

Republic of Botswana, 1966, *Transitional Plan for Economic and Social Development.* Gaborone: Government Printer.

Samatar, A. I., 1999, *An African Miracle: State and Class Leadership and Colonial Legacy in Botswana Development.* Portsmouth: Heinemann.

Schapera, I., 1955, *The Tswana.* London: Kegan Paul.

—, 1970, *Tribal Innovators: Tswana Chiefs and Social Change.* London: Anthlone Press.

—, 1994, *A Handbook of Tswana Law and Custom.* Gaborone: Botswana Society.

Sebudubudu, D., 2005, 'The Institutional Framework of the Developmental State in Botswana', in Mbabazi, P. and I. Taylor (eds), *The Potentiality of 'Developmental States' in Africa: Botswana and Uganda Compared.* Dakar: Codesria.

Somolekae, G., 1993, 'Bureaucracy and Democracy in Botswana: What type of a Relationship', in Stedman, S. (ed.), *Botswana: The Political Economy of Democratic Development.* Boulder: Lynne Rienner.

Taylor, I., 2003, 'The Developmental State in Africa: The Case of Botswana', paper presented to the Codesria Workshop on the Potentiality of Developmental States in Africa, Gaborone, 15–16 April.

Tordoff, W., 1997, *Government and Politics in Africa.* Basingstroke: Macmillan.

Tsie, B., 1998, 'The State and Development Policy in Botswana', in Hope, R.K. et al. (eds), *Public Administration and Policy in Botswana.* Cape Town: Juta & Co, Ltd.

Wallis, M., 1989, *Bureaucracy: Its Role in Third World Development.* Hong Kong: MacMillan.

Wiseman, J., 1977, 'Multi-Partyism in Africa: the case of Botswana', *African Affairs 76:* 303.

Interviews

(December 2008 and March 2009)

Mr Gobe Matenge, 19 December 2008

Kgosi Goboletswe Ketsitlile, 29 December 2008

Mr Otlaadisa Koosaletse, 31 December 2008

Hon. Peter Letlhogonolo Siele, 31 December 2008

Ms Tebelelo Seretse, 9 January 2009

Mr Botsweletse Kingsley Sebele, 10 January 2009

Dr Kesitegile Gobotswang, 15 January 2009

Dr Elmon Tafa, 2 February 2009

Mr Leach Tlhomelang, 3 February 2009

Mr Kentse Rammidi, 5 February 2009

Ms XYZ, 11 February 2009

Ms Festina Bakwena, 11 February 2009

Dr Patrick Molutsi, 22 February 2009

Ms Binkie Kerileng, 26 February 2009

Hon. Lt Gen. Mompati Merafhe, 9 March 2009

DISCUSSION PAPERS PUBLISHED BY THE INSTITUTE

Recent issues in the series are available electronically for download free of charge
www.nai.uu.se

1. Kenneth Hermele and Bertil Odén, *Sanctions and Dilemmas. Some Implications of Economic Sanctions against South Africa.* 1988. 43 pp. ISBN 91-7106-286-6

2. Elling Njål Tjønneland, *Pax Pretoriana. The Fall of Apartheid and the Politics of Regional Destabilisation.* 1989. 31 pp. ISBN 91-7106-292-0

3. Hans Gustafsson, Bertil Odén and Andreas Tegen, *South African Minerals. An Analysis of Western Dependence.* 1990. 47 pp. ISBN 91-7106-307-2

4. Bertil Egerö, *South African Bantustans. From Dumping Grounds to Battlefronts.* 1991. 46 pp. ISBN 91-7106-315-3

5. Carlos Lopes, *Enough is Enough! For an Alternative Diagnosis of the African Crisis.* 1994. 38 pp. ISBN 91-7106-347-1

6. Annika Dahlberg, *Contesting Views and Changing Paradigms.* 1994. 59 pp. ISBN 91-7106-357-9

7. Bertil Odén, *Southern African Futures. Critical Factors for Regional Development in Southern Africa.* 1996. 35 pp. ISBN 91-7106-392-7

8. Colin Leys and Mahmood Mamdani, *Crisis and Reconstruction – African Perspectives.* 1997. 26 pp. ISBN 91-7106-417-6

9. Gudrun Dahl, *Responsibility and Partnership in Swedish Aid Discourse.* 2001. 30 pp. ISBN 91-7106-473-7

10. Henning Melber and Christopher Saunders, *Transition in Southern Africa – Comparative Aspects.* 2001. 28 pp. ISBN 91-7106-480-X

11. *Regionalism and Regional Integration in Africa.* 2001. 74 pp. ISBN 91-7106-484-2

12. Souleymane Bachir Diagne, et al., *Identity and Beyond: Rethinking Africanity.* 2001. 33 pp. ISBN 91-7106-487-7

13. Georges Nzongola-Ntalaja, et al., *Africa in the New Millennium.* Edited by Raymond Suttner. 2001. 53 pp. ISBN 91-7106-488-5

14. *Zimbabwe's Presidential Elections 2002.* Edited by Henning Melber. 2002. 88 pp. ISBN 91-7106-490-7

15. Birgit Brock-Utne, *Language, Education and Democracy in Africa.* 2002. 47 pp. ISBN 91-7106-491-5

16. Henning Melber et al., *The New Partnership for Africa's development (NEPAD).* 2002. 36 pp. ISBN 91-7106-492-3

17. Juma Okuku, *Ethnicity, State Power and the Democratisation Process in Uganda.* 2002. 42 pp. ISBN 91-7106-493-1

18. Yul Derek Davids, et al., *Measuring Democracy and Human Rights in Southern Africa.* Compiled by Henning Melber. 2002. 50 pp. ISBN 91-7106-497-4

19. Michael Neocosmos, Raymond Suttner and Ian Taylor, *Political Cultures in Democratic South Africa.* Compiled by Henning Melber. 2002. 52 pp. ISBN 91-7106-498-2

20. Martin Legassick, *Armed Struggle and Democracy. The Case of South Africa.* 2002. 53 pp. ISBN 91-7106-504-0

21. Reinhart Kössler, Henning Melber and Per Strand, *Development from Below. A Namibian Case Study.* 2003. 32 pp. ISBN 91-7106-507-5

22. Fred Hendricks, *Fault-Lines in South African Democracy. Continuing Crises of Inequality and Injustice.* 2003. 32 pp. ISBN 91-7106-508-3

23. Kenneth Good, *Bushmen and Diamonds. (Un) Civil Society in Botswana.* 2003. 39 pp. ISBN 91-7106-520-2

24. Robert Kappel, Andreas Mehler, Henning Melber and Anders Danielson, *Structural Stability in an African Context.* 2003. 55 pp. ISBN 91-7106-521-0

25. Patrick Bond, *South Africa and Global Apartheid. Continental and International Policies and Politics.* 2004. 45 pp. ISBN 91-7106-523-7

26. Bonnie Campbell (ed.), *Regulating Mining in Africa. For whose benefit?* 2004. 89 pp. ISBN 91-7106-527-X

27. Suzanne Dansereau and Mario Zamponi, *Zimbabwe – The Political Economy of Decline.* Compiled by Henning Melber. 2005. 43 pp. ISBN 91-7106-541-5

28. Lars Buur and Helene Maria Kyed, *State Recognition of Traditional Authority in Mozambique. The nexus of Community Representation and State Assist-ance.*
2005. 30 pp. ISBN 91-7106-547-4

29. Hans Eriksson and Björn Hagströmer, *Chad – Towards Democratisation or Petro-Dictatorship?*
2005. 82 pp.ISBN 91-7106-549-

30. Mai Palmberg and Ranka Primorac (eds), *Skinning the Skunk – Facing Zimbabwean Futures.*
2005. 40 pp. ISBN 91-7106-552-0

31. Michael Brüntrup, Henning Melber and Ian Taylor, *Africa, Regional Cooperation and the World Market – Socio-Economic Strategies in Times of Global Trade Regimes.* Com-piled by Henning Melber.
2006. 70 pp. ISBN 91-7106-559-8

32. Fibian Kavulani Lukalo, *Extended Handshake or Wrestling Match? – Youth and Urban Culture Celebrating Politics in Kenya.*
2006.58 pp. ISBN 91-7106-567-9

33. Tekeste Negash, *Education in Ethiopia: From Crisis to the Brink of Collapse.*
2006. 55 pp. ISBN 91-7106-576-8

34. Fredrik Söderbaum and Ian Taylor (eds) *Micro-Regionalism in West Africa. Evidence from Two Case Studies.*
2006. 32 pp. ISBN 91-7106-584-9

35. Henning Melber (ed.), *On Africa – Scholars and African Studies.*
2006. 68 pp. ISBN 978-91-7106-585-8

36. Amadu Sesay, *Does One Size Fit All? The Sierra Leone Truth and Reconciliation Commission Revisited.*
2007. 56 pp. ISBN 978-91-7106-586-5

37. Karolina Hulterström, Amin Y. Kamete and Henning Melber, *Political Opposition in African Countries – The Case of Kenya, Namibia, Zambia and Zimbabwe.*
2007. 86 pp. ISBN 978-7106-587-2

38. Henning Melber (ed.), *Governance and State Delivery in Southern Africa. Examples from Botswana, Namibia and Zimbabwe.*
2007. 65 pp. ISBN 978-91-7106-587-2

39. Cyril Obi (ed.), *Perspectives on Côte d'Ivoire: Between Political Breakdown and Post-Conflict Peace.*
2007. 66 pp. ISBN 978-91-7106-606-6

40. Anna Chitando, *Imagining a Peaceful Society. A Vision of Children's Literature in a Post-Conflict Zimbabwe.*
2008. 26 pp. ISBN 978-91-7106-623-7

41. Olawale Ismail, *The Dynamics of Post-Conflict Reconstruction and Peace Building in West Africa. Between Change and Stability.*
2009.52 pp. ISBN 978-91-7106-637-4

42. Ron Sandrey and Hannah Edinger, *Examining the South Africa–China Agricultural Relationship.*
2009. 58 pp. ISBN 978-91-7106-643-5

43. Xuan Gao, *The Proliferation of Anti-Dumping and Poor Governance in Emerging Economies.*
2009. 41 pp. ISBN 978-91-7106-644-2

44. Lawal Mohammed Marafa, *Africa's Business and Development Relationship with China. Seeking Moral and Capital Values of the Last Economic Frontier.*
2009. xx pp. ISBN 978-91-7106-645-9

45. Mwangi wa Githinji, *Is That a Dragon or an Elephant on Your Ladder? The Potential Impact of China and India on Export Led Growth in African Countries.*
2009. 40 pp. ISBN 978-91-7106-646-6

46. Jo-Ansie van Wyk, *Cadres, Capitalists, Elites and Coalitions. The ANC, Business and Development in South Africa.*
2009. 61 pp. ISBN 978-91-7106-656-5

47. Elias Courson, *Movement for the Emancipation of the Niger Delta (MEND). Political Marginalization, Repression and Petro-Insurgency in the Niger Delta.*2009. 30 pp. ISBN 978-91-7106-657-2

48. Babatunde Ahonsi, *Gender Violence and HIV/AIDS in Post-Conflict West Africa. Issues and Responses.* 2010.
38 pp. ISBN 978-91-7106-665-7

49. Usman Tar and Abba Gana Shettima, *Endangered Democracy? The Struggle over Secularism and its Implications for Politics and Democracy in Nigeria.*
2010. 21 pp. ISBN 978-91-7106-666-4

50. Garth Andrew Myers, *Seven Themes in African Urban Dynamics.*2010. 28 pp.
ISBN 978-91-7106-677-0

51. Abdoumaliq Simone, *The Social Infrastructures of City Life in Contemporary Africa.*
2010. 33 pp. ISBN 978-91-7106-678-7

52. Li Anshan, *Chinese Medical Cooperation in Africa. With Special Emphasis on the Medical Teams and Anti-Malaria Campaign.*
2011. 24 pp. ISBN 978-91-7106-683-1

53. Folashade Hunsu, *Zangbeto: Navigating the Spaces Between Oral art, Communal Security And Conflict Mediation in Badagry, Nigeria.*
2011. 27 pp. ISBN 978-91-7106-688-6

54. Jeremiah O. Arowosegbe, *Reflections on the Challenge of Reconstructing Post-Conflict States in West Africa: Insights from Claude Ake's Political Writings.*
2011. 40 pp. ISBN 978-91-7106-689-3

55. Bertil Odén, *The Africa Policies of Nordic Countries and the Erosion of the Nordic Aid Model: A comparative study.*
2011. 66 pp. ISBN 978-91-7106-691-6

56. Angela Meyer, *Peace and Security Cooperation in Central Africa: Developments, Challenges and Prospects.*
2011. 47 pp ISBN 978-91-7106-693-0

57. Godwin R. Murunga, *Spontaneous or Premeditated? Post-Election Violence in Kenya.*
2011. 58 pp. ISBN 978-91-7106-694-7

58. David Sebudubudu & Patrick Molutsi, *The Elite as a Critical Factor in National Development: The Case of Botswana.*
2011. 48 pp. ISBN 978-91-7106-695-4

www.ingramcontent.com/pod-product-compliance
Lightning Source LLC
Chambersburg PA
CBHW080209300326
41934CB00039B/3432